# SCHOLASTIC

# Scholastic Success With
# Fluency

## Grade 3

by Linda Van Vickle

New York • Toronto • London • Auckland • Sydney
Mexico City • New Delhi • Hong Kong • Buenos Aires

**Teaching** *Resources*

Cover art by Amy Vangsgard
Cover design by Maria Lilja
Interior illustrations by Milton Hall
Interior design by Quack & Company

ISBN 0-439-55387-3

Copyright © 2004 Scholastic, Inc.
All rights reserved. Printed in the U.S.A.

1 2 3 4 5 6 7 8 9 10    40    09 08 07 06 05 04

# Introduction

*Parents and teachers alike will find this book a valuable tool in helping students become fluent readers. Fluency is the ability to read smoothly and easily and is essential to reading comprehension. Prereading activities, which include building vocabulary and context, help students prepare for the readings. Decoding words ahead of time enables students to focus more attention on the actual meaning of the text. Activities are also designed to help students build their reading speed. By training their eyes to read more than one word at a time, students stay more focused and can better remember what they have read. This book also encourages students to read aloud with expression, which helps foster better comprehension. Students demonstrate their understanding of the readings in follow-up exercises and then extend this understanding through critical thinking questions. You will feel rewarded providing such a valuable resource for your students. Remember to praise them for their efforts and successes!*

# Table of Contents

# Make It a Jumbo!

 **Building Vocabulary**

Did you know that the English language is growing? Each year new words are added to the dictionary. You are going to read the story of how one word became part of the English language. The word is *jumbo*.

Have you heard or used this word before? Write down what you think it means.

_____

_____

The words below are all used to describe the main character in the story. Show that you know the meanings of these words by using them to fill in the blanks of the sentences that follow.

**famous          star          celebrity          popularity**

**1.** The _ _ _ _ of the show was a _ _ _ _ _ _   _ ☐ _ ☐ _ _ _ _ _ .

**2.** His ☐ _ _ _ _ _ _ _ _ _ _ made the show a big success.

The words below help tell about the places the main character has been. Use these words to complete the sentences that follow.

**London     train     United States     Natural History Museum**

**Canada     circus     Tufts University**

**3.** The animals in a _ _ _ _ _ _ _ often travel

by ☐ _ _ _ _ from city to city.

**4.** ☐ _ _ _ _ _ _ is the capital city of England.

**5.** The three countries that make up North America are Mexico,

_ _ _ _ _ _ _ , and the _ _ _ _ _ _ _ _ _ ☐ _ _ _ _ .

**6.** The _ _ _ _ _ _ _ _ ☐ _ _ _ _ _ _ _ _ _ _ _ _
is in Washington, D.C.

**7.** _ _ _ _ _ _ _ ☐ _ _ _ _ _ _ _ _ _ is in the state of Massachusetts.

Unscramble the letters in the boxes to find out about the main character of this story. The main character is an _ _ _ _ _ _ _ _ _ _ .

**Building Vocabulary**—*Many words in the story are compound words. A* **compound word** *is a word made by joining two words together.*

Write the two words that make up each of the following compound words you will read in the story.

something     _____     _____

showman      _____     _____

railroad       _____     _____

everyone      _____     _____

anything      _____     _____

Before you begin reading "Make It a Jumbo," practice reading some of the words from the story.

| accident | tons | tunnels | hundred |
|---|---|---|---|
| railroad | palace | famous | display |
| Canada | circus | tragedy | celebrity |
| zoo | popularity | skeleton | millions |
| track | United States | London | largest |
| language | anything | showman | elephant |

1. Color the three boxes that contain the names of cities or countries red.

2. Color the three boxes containing words relating to trains yellow.

3. Color the four boxes containing words relating to size or numbers blue.

4. What two words name places where you might find an elephant?

   _____     _____

5. What three words suggest this story may not have a happy ending?

   _____     _____     _____

6. Outline the three boxes containing compound words in green.

➡️ **Reading the Story**

Have you ever ridden on a *jumbo* jet or ordered a *jumbo*-sized pizza or soft drink? You may have eaten *jumbo* shrimp or looked at something that seemed extra large and said, "That's a *jumbo*!" You may not know how the word *jumbo* became part of the English language. It was originally the name of a very big and very famous elephant.

In 1882, Jumbo, the African elephant, was the star of the London Zoo. Jumbo was said to be the largest elephant in the world. He stood more than 11 feet tall and weighed seven tons. Visitors to the zoo loved Jumbo, but zookeepers were afraid that Jumbo was too big and could cause an accident.

The great circus showman P.T. Barnum offered to buy Jumbo for $10,000. The London Zoo accepted the offer and sent Jumbo to America. For the next three years, Jumbo toured the United States and Canada and became the biggest celebrity in the circus. Jumbo traveled on the circus train in a specially built palace car. Barnum told everyone to come see Jumbo before he grew too big to go through the train tunnels and could no longer travel with the circus. Millions of people paid to see the world's biggest elephant.

In 1885, at the peak of Jumbo's popularity, tragedy struck. While the circus was in Canada, Jumbo was standing on a railroad track when an oncoming train struck him. The train was knocked off the tracks, and Jumbo was killed.

This was not the end of Jumbo. His skeleton was given to the Museum of Natural History in Washington, D.C. His hide was stuffed and put on display at Tufts University. Most importantly, people remembered Jumbo and began calling anything larger than normal *jumbo*-sized. Over a hundred years later, *jumbo* is still part of the English language.

**Thinking About the Story**

1. Visitors to the London Zoo loved Jumbo, but the zookeepers were afraid of him. Why do you think these two groups of people saw Jumbo in very different ways?

   _____

   _____

   _____

   _____

2. Jumbo was killed at the "peak" of his popularity. What does *peak* mean?

   _____

   _____

3. Why do you think a museum and a university would want Jumbo's remains?

   _____

   _____

   _____

4. P.T. Barnum was a great showman and promoter. When he displayed Jumbo, he showed him with a tiny albino elephant named Tom Thumb. This made Jumbo look even bigger. After Jumbo was killed, Barnum brought his mate over from the London Zoo and displayed her as "Jumbo's widow" alongside Jumbo's stuffed hide. Barnum made over one million dollars on his $10,000 investment in Jumbo! On another piece of paper, design an advertisement P.T. Barnum might have placed in a newspaper to get the crowds out to see Jumbo.

 Other words in the English language come from names, many of them the names of people. These kinds of words are called *eponyms*. Choose one of the following words and research the person whose name it came from: boycott, braille, bloomers, cardigan, diesel, guillotine, leotard, maverick, pasteurize, or sandwich.

Name _____

# Against the Odds

 **Building Vocabulary**

"Since we have won all of our games this season, the odds of our team winning the championship game are very good," said the coach.

"Since you have not studied, your odds of passing the test are not very good," the teacher told the student.

In both of these statements, the word *odds* refers to how likely it is for something to happen. Read each of the following statements and then circle whether you think the odds are good—something will probably happen—or the odds are not good—something will not likely happen.

1. **Every Tuesday so far this year, the cafeteria has served pizza. Next Tuesday, the cafeteria will probably serve pizza.**

    The odds are   good / not good.

2. **Our school has sold 500 raffle tickets, and I bought one. I will win the raffle.**

    The odds are   good / not good.

3. **I am going to a baseball game at Yankee Stadium. I brought my glove because I am going to catch a fly ball.**

    The odds are   good / not good.

4. **Ten kids in my class have the flu. My mom, dad, and sister have the flu. My stomach is starting to feel funny. I think I am getting the flu.**

    The odds are   good / not good.

Think about a person who wants to be a successful athlete. What do you think will give that person "good odds" at being successful?

_____

_____

_____

Scholastic Teaching Resources

**Building Vocabulary**

You are going to be reading the story of Wilma Rudolph, the first American woman to win three gold medals in the Olympics. When you read about her life, you will see that when she was born, her odds of growing up to achieve this success were not very good.

Here are two lists of words you will find in this story. One list contains words that relate to all the obstacles Wilma had to overcome. The other list contains words that relate to how Wilma overcame these obstacles. Practice reading the words in each list.

| | |
|---|---|
| premature | segregation |
| crutches | deformed |
| incurable | sickly |
| crippled | |

| | |
|---|---|
| encouragement | excelled |
| championship | talent |
| determination | |

Use the words from the two lists to complete the puzzle.

**Across**

1. disabled or lame

4. weak, unhealthy

7. born in less than normal time

9. supports used for walking

10. support or inspiration

12. did better than others

**Down**

2. not able to be cured

3. the practice of separating by race

5. misshapen

6. strong will

8. a competition to determine a winner

11. special ability

**Reading the Story**

Not many people would have thought that Wilma Rudolph would grow up to be the first American woman to win three gold medals in the Olympics. Not many people even thought baby Wilma would live to grow up. Wilma beat the odds to not only grow up, but to grow up to be great.

Wilma was born in 1940 to a poor African-American family in Tennessee. She was the twentieth of twenty-two children. Wilma was born premature and was a tiny, sickly baby. Because of the segregation laws of that time, Wilma could not even be treated at the local hospital. It accepted only white patients. Wilma's mother did not give up and nursed her baby through illness after illness. With her mother's help, Wilma beat the odds and survived.

When Wilma's left foot became weak and deformed, her mother took her to the doctor. Wilma had polio, an incurable disease that often crippled those who had it. Again, Wilma's mother did not give up. She found a black medical college and for two years drove 50 miles twice a week, so Wilma could receive treatment. At home, Wilma's brothers and sisters helped her with exercises to make her leg and foot strong. With their encouragement, Wilma worked hard and did not give up. When she was 12 years old, she could walk without crutches or a brace. She beat the odds a second time.

In school, Wilma joined the basketball team, but for three years the coach did not put her in a single game. During her sophomore year, she finally became a starting guard and excelled. She went on to set state records for scoring and led her team to a state championship. Wilma caught the attention of a college track coach who invited her to attend a summer sports camp. Wilma discovered that she had a talent for running. Her speed carried her to her first Olympic Games in 1956. She was only 16 years old when she won a bronze medal. Four years later, Wilma returned to the Olympics, this time winning three gold medals.

From a tiny baby no one thought would live, to a little girl no one thought would walk, to a world class athlete—Wilma Rudolph showed how with hard work and determination a person could beat the odds.

Scholastic Teaching Resources

Name _____        Against the Odds

  **Thinking About the Story**

Use words from the story to complete the following sentences.

Wilma did not have very good odds of becoming a famous and successful athlete because of the following reasons.

1. She was born _ _ _ _ _ _ _ _ _ and was a _ _ _ _ _ _ baby.

2. Because of _ _ _ _ _ _ _ _ _ _ _ _ laws, Wilma could not get treatment at a local hospital.

3. The disease _ _ _ _ _ left Wilma's foot _ _ _ _ _ _ _ _.

Wilma was also a poor African-American girl. Why might this also have hurt Wilma's chances to become a successful athlete in the 1940s and 1950s?

_____

_____

_____

_____

Wilma beat the odds and went on not only to become a successful athlete, but also to work to end segregation and to improve opportunities for women in sports. What did each of the following people do to help Wilma succeed?

**her mother** _____

_____

**her brothers and sisters** _____

_____

**her coaches** _____

_____

What do you think Wilma herself had to do to beat the odds against her and become successful?

_____

_____

_____

Scholastic Teaching Resources

# Wet and Wild Fall

 **Building Vocabulary**

You are going to read about some amazing waterfall adventures. Before you read, you will find it helpful to know and practice some of the words from the story. The first word is *waterfall*. It is a **compound word**. The two words that make it up are ＿ ＿ ＿ ＿ ＿ and ＿ ＿ ＿ ＿. When *water* flowing from a river reaches a cliff, it *falls* over it. One of the most famous waterfalls in the world is Niagara Falls in New York.

Here are some of the other words you will find in the story. Practice reading them several times.

| | | | | |
|---|---|---|---|---|
| Niagara Falls | stunt | New York | gallons | United States |
| cannon | brink | rapids | miracle | Horseshoe Falls |
| Canada | oak | wonders | daredevils | schoolteacher |
| adventure | barrel | July | Michigan | forbidding |

Match each word with its definition. Use a dictionary for help.

**a.** forbidding      ____ **an unexplainable event**

**b.** stunt      ____ **the very edge**

**c.** daredevil      ____ **not allowing**

**d.** miracle      ____ **a risky act**

**e.** brink      ____ **one who takes risks**

What kind of *stunt* might a *daredevil* perform using an *oak barrel* and a *waterfall*?

_____

_____

Scholastic Teaching Resources

**Building Speed**

Imagine you come to school one day and when your teacher begins to talk, she pauses for a second or two after every word:

> "Good    morning    class.    Today    we    are    going    to    learn    about    the    states    and    their    capitals.    Then    in    math,    we    will    begin    working    on    multiplication."

Can you imagine how long the day would seem if she continued to talk so slowly? You would have a very hard time paying attention. Your mind would begin to wander, and you would start to think about other things and not even hear or remember what your teacher said.

Your mind reacts the same way when you read too slowly. It starts to lose interest in what you are reading, and soon you find you cannot remember something you just read! Building your reading speed will not only help you read faster, but will help you stay more focused on what you read. Being more focused will help you better remember what you read.

You can become a faster reader by training your eyes to see or to scan more than one word at a time. Practice doing this as you read about some waterfall adventures. Try to read each line of the story at once rather than each individual word.

Niagara Falls
in New York
is one of
the world's wonders.
The falls sit
on the border between
the United States and Canada,
and there are
separate falls
in each country.
The U.S. Niagara Falls
is 180 feet tall.
The Canadian Falls,
also called Horseshoe Falls,
is 170 feet tall.
Each minute
about 35 million
gallons of water

thunder over the tops
of these waterfalls.

Can you imagine
that anyone would want
to go over the top
of huge waterfalls like these?
Over the years,
there have been daredevils
who took the risk
and some who went
over the falls by accident.
Not everyone lived
to tell about the adventure,
but some survived
the wet and wild fall.

Scholastic Teaching Resources

The first person
to go over Horseshoe Falls
in a barrel
was Annie Taylor,
a schoolteacher from Michigan.
Miss Taylor had a lot
of bills to pay, and she hoped
her trip over the falls
would make her
a lot of money.
On October 24, 1901,
she climbed into an oak barrel
and went over Horseshoe Falls.
Everyone was amazed
that she lived.
She had a small cut
on her head
and was very frightened
when she climbed
out of the barrel.
But otherwise, she was fine.
When asked if she would ever
perform such a stunt again,
Miss Taylor said
she would rather stand
in front of a loaded cannon
than make another trip
over the falls.
Miss Taylor never did earn
any money for her stunt.

Over the years,
as more people
were hurt or killed
from trying to go over the falls,
the United States and Canada
passed laws forbidding such stunts.
But accidents do happen,

and one accident
led to what some call
the "miracle at the falls."

On July 9, 1960,
seven-year-old Roger Woodward
and his sister, Deane,
fell out of a boat
that had become caught
in the rapids above Horseshoe Falls.
Deane was able to swim
close enough to the edge
for tourists to grab her hands
and pull her out.
She was only 15 feet
from the brink of the falls.
Roger was not so lucky.
The little boy
was swept over the top
of the 170-foot waterfall.

Passengers in the tour boats
at the base of the falls
could not believe their eyes
when they saw Roger
pop up out of the water.
They threw him a life preserver
and pulled him
onto the deck of the boat.
Roger had only a few scratches.
He went over
the huge waterfall
wearing only a life jacket.
He managed to avoid hitting
all the huge rocks
at the base of the falls.
It really was a miracle
that Roger survived
his wet and wild fall.

Think about how your eyes moved when you read the story this way. Were you able to read the entire line at once? Did it help knowing the meanings of the words used in the story? What did you find most helped you read and understand this story?

_____

_____

_____

After reading the story the first time, what do you most remember about it?

_____

_____

Now read the story again on page 16 in the form that it would take in a book. See if you can still scan more than one word at a time when you read.

**Thinking About the Story**

1. **Miss Taylor went over the falls to make money to pay her bills. What other reasons might people have for attempting such a dangerous stunt?**

    _____

    _____

    _____

2. **Miss Taylor and Roger Woodward both survived their trips over the falls.**

    **How were their trips different?** _____

    _____

    _____

    **How were they similar?** _____

    _____

    _____

3. **It is now illegal to try to go over Niagara Falls. If someone wants to take a chance and perform a dangerous stunt, do you think there should be laws to prevent them? Why or why not? Write your answer on another sheet of paper.**

### Reading the Story

Niagara Falls in New York is one of the world's wonders. The falls sit on the border between the United States and Canada, and there are separate falls in each country. The U.S. Niagara Falls is about 180 feet tall. The Canadian Falls, also called Horseshoe Falls, is about 170 feet tall. Each minute about 35 million gallons of water thunder over the tops of these waterfalls.

Can you imagine that anyone would want to go over the top of huge waterfalls like these? Over the years, there have been daredevils who took the risk and some who went over the falls by accident. Not everyone lived to tell about the adventure, but some survived the wet and wild fall.

The first person to go over Horseshoe Falls in a barrel was Annie Taylor, a schoolteacher from Michigan. Miss Taylor had a lot of bills to pay, and she hoped her trip over the falls would make her a lot of money. On October 24, 1901, she climbed into an oak barrel and went over Horseshoe Falls. Everyone was amazed that she lived. She had a small cut on her head and was very frightened when she climbed out of the barrel. But otherwise, she was fine. When asked if she would ever perform such a stunt again, Miss Taylor said she would rather stand in front of a loaded cannon than make another trip over the falls. Miss Taylor never did earn any money for her stunt.

Over the years, as more people were hurt or killed from trying to go over the falls, the United States and Canada passed laws forbidding such stunts. But accidents do happen, and one accident led to what some call the "miracle at the falls."

On July 9, 1960, seven-year-old Roger Woodward and his sister, Deane, fell out of a boat that had become caught in the rapids above Horseshoe Falls. Deane was able to swim close enough to the edge for tourists to grab her hands and pull her out. She was only 15 feet from the brink of the falls. Roger was not so lucky. The little boy was swept over the top of the 170-foot waterfall.

Passengers in the tour boats at the base of the falls could not believe their eyes when they saw Roger pop up out of the water. They threw him a life preserver and pulled him onto the deck of the boat. Roger had only a few scratches. He went over the huge waterfall wearing only a life jacket. He managed to avoid hitting all the huge rocks at the base of the falls. It really was a miracle that Roger survived his wet and wild fall.

Scholastic Teaching Resources

# Daisy Goes to School

**Building Vocabulary**

You can tell from the title that this story is going to be about school. Many of the words used in the story relate to school. Practice reading this list of words. See how fast you can go.

**school     lunchroom     desk     playground     classroom     recess**

This story is also about Daisy, a special visitor to the school. Use the clues below to fill in the blanks. The answer will tell you something about who Daisy is.

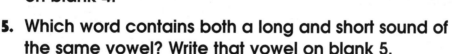

1    2    3    4    5      6    7    8

**1.** Which compound word describes where you play during recess? Write the first letter of the second part of the compound word on blank 1.

**2.** Where do you eat at school? Write the second letter of that word on blank 2.

**3.** What vowel is not found in any of the words? Write it on blank 3.

**4.** Where do you spend most of your time working when you are in a classroom? Write the first letter of that word on blank 4.

**5.** Which word contains both a long and short sound of the same vowel? Write that vowel on blank 5.

**6.** Which consonant ends the word that describes where you play the most? Write that consonant on blank 6.

**7.** Which vowel occurs most often in the list of words? Write it on blank 7.

**8.** The same letter that begins the first word in this answer ends the second word. Write it on blank 8.

**Now you know who Daisy is!**

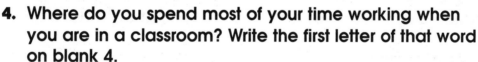

**Daisy Goes to School**

➡️ **Building Vocabulary**

You are going to read about Daisy, a guide dog. Guide dogs help people who are blind become more independent by helping them avoid obstacles when they walk. For example, a guide dog can lead its owner to a street corner or to the foot of a flight of stairs. Guide dogs are very special because of the responsibilities they have for their owners' safety.

A guide dog must be carefully trained to handle these responsibilities. What do you think a guide dog must be trained to do and not to do?

_____

_____

_____

_____

_____

Guide dog owners also have special responsibilities toward their dogs. You will read about the relationship between a guide dog, Daisy, and her owner, Ann. Before you begin reading, think about what Daisy must do for her owner, Ann, and what Ann must do for Daisy. Read each phrase below and write *Daisy* if it describes what Daisy must do and *Ann* if it describes what Ann must do. Write *both* if the action describes what Ann and Daisy must both do.

**follow basic commands** _____

**pay close attention** _____

**not get distracted** _____

**attend special classes** _____

**communicate** _____

**practice** _____

**show love and affection** _____

Name _____

 **Building Speed**—*Reading more than one word at a time allows you to read faster, which can keep you more interested in what you are reading.*

Practice expanding the number of words your eye scans as you read about Daisy for the first time.

Every school day,
Ann takes her dog, Daisy,
with her to school.
Daisy sits next to Ann
while she works
at her desk.
If Ann goes
to another classroom,
Daisy goes with her.
Daisy even goes with Ann
to the lunchroom
and then out
to the playground
for recess.
Not every dog
can go to school,
but Daisy is not
an ordinary dog.
Daisy is a guide dog.
Ann is blind
and uses Daisy's help
to safely move
around the school.

Ann and Daisy learned
to be a good team.
When Daisy was a puppy,
she was taught
to follow basic commands.
She had to learn
to always pay close attention
and not to be distracted.
A guide dog cannot

just leave its owner
to chase a car
or to get attention
from other people.
After Daisy was trained,
she was introduced to Ann,
and together they attended
special classes.
Ann had to learn
different commands,
using her voice
and body movements,
to tell Daisy
what Ann needed her to do.
Once Ann and Daisy could
communicate with each other,
they had to practice
walking together
until Daisy became familiar
with Ann's home,
neighborhood, and school.

Ann and Daisy each
have responsibilities.
Ann must always keep up
Daisy's training
and practice with her.

She has to make sure that Daisy
receives good health care
and is always well fed
and well groomed.
It is very important
that Ann shows Daisy
lots of love
and affection, too.
Happy guide dogs
always work best.
In return, Daisy gives Ann
more freedom to move around.
She helps Ann
avoid obstacles
and find doors and stairs.
She can help Ann cross streets.
Ann can walk faster

and feel safer
when she is with Daisy.
Sometimes people ask Ann
questions about Daisy.
Ann has met new people
and made new friends this way.
While Ann is at school,
she works hard at her lessons.
Daisy is working hard, too.
She is carefully following
Ann's commands,
so Ann can move safely
around the school.
Together, they make a great team.

Answer the questions below to see how well
you remember what you just read.

**Ann and Daisy had to learn how to work
together. What did Daisy have to learn when
she was a puppy?**

_____

_____

_____

**What did Ann have to learn so she could work with Daisy?**

_____

_____

**When were Ann and Daisy able to practice walking together?**

_____

_____

Now read the story of Ann and Daisy again the way it might appear in a book. See
if you were able to answer all of the questions correctly. Make any corrections.

**Reading the Story**

Every school day, Ann takes her dog, Daisy, with her to school. Daisy sits next to Ann while she works at her desk. If Ann goes to another classroom, Daisy goes with her. Daisy even goes with Ann to the lunchroom and then out to the playground for recess. Not every dog can go to school, but Daisy is not an ordinary dog. Daisy is a guide dog. Ann is blind and uses Daisy's help to safely move around the school.

Ann and Daisy learned to be a good team. When Daisy was a puppy, she was taught to follow basic commands. She had to learn to always pay close attention and not to be distracted. A guide dog cannot just leave its owner to chase a car or to get attention from other people. After Daisy was trained, she was introduced to Ann, and together they attended special classes. Ann had to learn different commands, using her voice and body movements, to tell Daisy what she needed Daisy to do. Once Ann and Daisy could communicate with each other, they had to practice walking together until Daisy became familiar with Ann's home, neighborhood, and school.

Ann and Daisy each have responsibilities. Ann must always keep up Daisy's training and practice with her. She has to make sure that Daisy receives good health care and is always well fed and well groomed. It is very important that Ann shows Daisy lots of love and affection, too. Happy guide dogs always work best. In return, Daisy gives Ann more freedom to move around. She helps Ann avoid obstacles and find doors and stairs. She can help Ann cross streets. Ann can walk faster and feel safer when she is with Daisy. Sometimes people ask Ann questions about Daisy. Ann has met new people and made new friends this way.

While Ann is at school, she works hard at her lessons. Daisy is working hard, too. She is carefully following Ann's commands, so Ann can move safely around the school. Together, they make a great team.

# Letter From the Fair

 **Building Context: Content—**_One of the ways to become a better reader is to gain some understanding of the subject before beginning to read a passage. This provides a context or a base on which to build an understanding of what is to be read._

Have you ever attended a city fair or a state fair? What do you think happens at a fair?

_____

_____

You are going to read a letter about a world's fair that took place about a hundred years ago in St. Louis, Missouri. The 1904 St. Louis World's Fair was the biggest and most spectacular fair of its time, and many say no fair has ever been better. There were over 1,500 buildings at the fair and 75 miles of sidewalks and roads. Displays set up by 62 countries and 43 states showed all the cultural and technological achievements of the time. Here are some of the special features of the fair that you will read about in the letter.

**Palaces:** There were 12 huge buildings with massive columns and towers. Each one contained exhibits on a particular theme such as transportation, art, education, and agriculture. A very popular palace was the Palace of Electricity. Thomas Edison himself helped set it up. Do you know who Thomas Edison was? Why do you think this palace was so popular at this time?

_____

_____

**Olympics:** The 1904 Olympic Games were held in St. Louis. Have you seen the Olympic Games on television? What do you know about them?

_____

_____

**The Pike:** This was a mile-long strip of rides, restaurants, and exhibits. Many countries reproduced miniature landscapes along the Pike. For example, visitors could visit a temple from Asia, an Irish village, and even the Swiss Alps! Many new foods were introduced for the first time at the fair and went on to become very popular. You have, no doubt, eaten them yourself. Guess what some of these foods might have been. (One of them is something you like when it is hot.)

_____

_____

Scholastic Teaching Resources

**Reading the Story**

As you read about the St. Louis World's Fair, continue to practice expanding your eye scan, so you can read more quickly.

July 5, 1904

Dear Aunt Carol,

    Mother, Father, and I are having a great time at the World's Fair in St. Louis. I want to tell you what we have seen so far.

    The fair is so big! It covers more than 1,200 acres and is like a small city. There are 12 huge buildings called palaces that hold all kinds of exhibits. Mother enjoyed the Palace of Art, and Father learned a lot at the Palace of Agriculture. My favorite was the Palace of Electricity. You would not believe how bright electric lights can be. I found out that the great inventor Thomas Edison himself helped to set up the exhibits in this palace.

    Yesterday, Father and I watched some of the Olympic Games. Did you know this is the first time the games have been held in this country? Some events were held in a concrete stadium. Father said it is the first concrete stadium in the United States.

    In the afternoon, we like to walk along the Pike. What amazing sights there are! We took a boat ride and went under a 40-foot waterfall. There is an Eskimo village with real Eskimos and their dogs. There are other villages from all around the world. We also went ice-skating during a snowstorm. I don't know how that could happen in July, but it did! We saw a new invention called a "moving picture," and it was amazing. I hope you can see a moving picture someday.

    You know I like to eat, and the food here has been very good and very different. I ate a hot dog, but don't worry. It is not really a dog. It is more like a sausage. Mother tried a new drink called iced tea and really liked it. Father and I tried a new health food called peanut butter. It was good, but it stuck to the roof of my mouth. My favorite food is called an ice-cream cone. It is sweet and cold and delicious.

    We have spent a week at the fair, and there is still so much to see. I will tell you more about it when we get home.

Your nephew,

Tom

**Thinking About the Story**

**1.** If you had not already known the fair took place a hundred years ago, what are some of the clues in the letter that let you know?

_____

_____

_____

_____

**2.** What do you think a "moving picture" is?

_____

_____

**3.** Thinking about all the sights Tom described, which do you think you would like to have seen the most? Why?

_____

_____

_____

**4.** There were many "firsts" at the 1904 World's Fair. Name three of them.

_____

_____

 **On another sheet of paper, draw a picture of one of the sights Tom describes in his letter.**

Scholastic Teaching Resources

Name _____

# Let's Recycle!

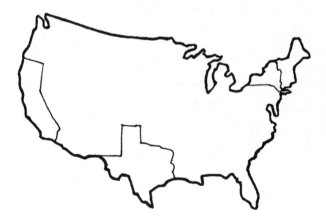

**Building Vocabulary and Context**

You are going to read an article about recycling. What do you already know about recycling? Does your family recycle?

_____

_____

How do you think recycling helps the environment?

_____

_____

_____

Practice reading some of the words you will find in the article. Read through the following chart several times, trying to increase your speed each time.

| | | |
|---|---|---|
| aluminum | paper | commercial |
| California | Texas | household |
| television | airlines | pollutants |
| resources | glass | New York |
| plastic | natural | containers |
| | landfill | |

Use the chart to answer each question.

**1.** What four words name materials that might be recycled?

_____  _____  _____

**2.** Which three states will be mentioned in the article? Circle the name of the largest of those three states.

_____  _____  _____

**3.** Which word names a place where trash and garbage are dumped?

_____

**Building Speed**

Keeping the earth clean
and protecting its resources
is a big job, but everybody can help.
One easy way is to recycle.
If every household recycled
aluminum, glass, plastic, and paper,
we could save natural resources
and help clean up the earth.
Does your family
recycle aluminum cans?
Enough aluminum is thrown away
in the United States
to rebuild our fleet
of commercial airlines
four times every year!
Recycling just one aluminum can
saves enough energy
to run a television set for three hours.
So instead of tossing
those soft drink cans in the trash,
take them to a recycling center.
    Did you know that
over 41 billion glass containers
are made each year?
How many of these
does your family use and recycle?
Maybe you do not use much glass,
but recycling just one glass container
can save enough energy
to light a 10-watt light bulb
for four hours.
Every ton of glass
made from recycled materials
can save 250 pounds of mining waste.

    Maybe you use
more plastic than glass.
Plastic can be recycled, too!
Each year in the United States,
we use enough plastic wrap
to wrap up the whole state of Texas.
If we recycled every plastic bottle,
we could keep two billion tons
of plastic out of landfills.
    It is not hard to recycle paper,
and that, too, can make
a big difference.
Every year enough paper
is thrown away to make
a 12-foot wall that stretches
from New York to California.
Instead of building paper walls
and filling landfills, let's recycle!
Each pound of recycled paper
keeps six pounds of pollutants
out of our air.
A ton of recycled paper
saves 17 trees
and 7,000 gallons of water.
    Let's all try to clean up the earth
and save its resources.
Start by recycling at home.
Tell your neighbors about recycling.
Maybe you could start
a recycling club at school.
We can all do our part to keep
the earth clean
and protect
its resources.

Scholastic Teaching Resources

 **Reading the Story**

Keeping the earth clean and protecting its resources is a big job, but everybody can help. One easy way is to recycle. If every household recycled aluminum, glass, plastic, and paper, we could save natural resources and help clean up the earth. Does your family recycle aluminum cans? Enough aluminum is thrown away in the United States to rebuild our fleet of commercial airlines four times every year! Recycling just one aluminum can saves enough energy to run a television set for three hours. So instead of tossing those soft drink cans in the trash, take them to a recycling center.

Did you know that over 41 billion glass containers are made each year? How many of these does your family use and recycle? Maybe you do not use much glass, but recycling just one glass container can save enough energy to light a 10-watt light bulb for four hours. Every ton of glass made from recycled materials can save 250 pounds of mining waste.

Maybe you use more plastic than glass. Plastic can be recycled, too! Each year in the United States, we use enough plastic wrap to wrap up the whole state of Texas. If we recycled every plastic bottle, we could keep two billion tons of plastic out of landfills.

It is not hard to recycle paper, and that, too, can make a big difference. Every year enough paper is thrown away to make a 12-foot wall that stretches from New York to California. Instead of building paper walls and filling landfills, let's recycle! Each pound of recycled paper keeps six pounds of pollutants out of our air. A ton of recycled paper saves 17 trees and 7,000 gallons of water.

Let's all try to clean up the earth and save its resources. Start by recycling at home. Tell your neighbors about recycling. Maybe you could start a recycling club at school. We can all do our part to keep the earth clean and protect its resources.

Name _____

 **Thinking About the Writer's Purpose—**
*Writers may have several reasons for writing. The most common reasons are to inform, to persuade, and to entertain. A writer who wants to* **inform** *presents information you may not already know. A writer who wants to* **persuade** *tries to convince you to take some sort of action. A writer who wants to* **entertain** *presents material that is funny or interesting.*

**1.** The main purpose of "Let's Recycle" is to persuade the readers to do what?

_____

_____

**2.** Keeping the earth __ __ __ __ __ and protecting its

__ __ __ __ __ __ __ __ __ are two main reasons to recycle.

**3.** In order to persuade the readers, the writer includes some specific information about the benefits of recycling. Give two examples of facts you learned in reading this article.

_____

_____

_____

_____

**4.** The writer also tries to make the article entertaining by using facts that are surprising or interesting. Give two examples of details that you think the writer included to make the article entertaining as well as persuasive and informative.

_____

_____

_____

_____

Name _____

# A Greedy Frog

## (A Tale From Australia)

 **Building Vocabulary**

The story you will read is from Australia, a continent and country that lies southeast of Asia between the Pacific and Indian oceans. Most of central Australia is a desert, where water is scarce and therefore precious.

There are several animals in this story, some of which are found only in Australia. Write the letter of each animal's description next to its picture.

**a.** eel—a long, snakelike fish

**b.** emu—a large, flightless bird

**c.** frog—an amphibian with webbed feet and long hind legs suited for leaping

**d.** kangaroo—an animal with large hind legs used for jumping

**e.** kookaburra— a kingfisher bird, known for its call that sounds like laughter

**f.** lizard—a reptile having a long scaly body, four legs, and a tail

**g.** wombat—an animal resembling a small bear

1. _____

2. _____

3. _____

4. _____

5. _____

6. _____

7. _____

Name _____

   **Reading the Story**

Tiddalik was the biggest frog in the world. One day he woke up and felt very thirsty. So he began to drink and drink and drink. Tiddalik did not stop drinking until he drank up all the water in the world. All the lakes, rivers, ponds, and streams were empty!

Soon all the other plants and animals began to grow thirsty because there was no water. It was all inside greedy Tiddalik. When the plants and trees began to die, the animals knew something had to be done. They called for a meeting to talk about ways to make Tiddalik give back the water.

All day they talked, but they could not agree on a plan. Then a wise wombat came up with an idea. He said that the animals should find a way to make Tiddalik laugh. Once the big frog started laughing, all the water would pour from his mouth. There would then be plenty of water for all the plants and trees and animals. Everyone agreed that the wombat had come up with a good plan.

However, making Tiddalik laugh was not so easy. The noisy kookaburra bird told its best jokes, but Tiddalik did not laugh. Lizard did a funny waddle back and forth, but Tiddalik did not laugh. Kangaroo did backward flips, but Tiddalik did not laugh. The emu fluffed its feathers and wiggled its toes, but Tiddalik did not laugh. The poor animals were tired and thirsty and ready to give up trying to make the greedy frog laugh.

Hearing all the joking and wondering why the creek was so dry, an eel wiggled out from under a rock. The eel did not know what had happened, but it knew it needed to find some water. So it crawled out of the dry creek and then tried to hop on the end of his tail toward the sounds of all the animals.

Eel had never tried to stand on the end of its tail before, and when it reached the animals, it was wobbling this way and that way. It hopped and twisted and

turned to try to keep its balance. When Tiddalik saw the poor eel twisting and turning and hopping, the frog could hold back no longer. Tiddalik burst out laughing.

The water gushed out of Tiddalik's mouth and filled the lakes, rivers, ponds, and streams. All the world had water again.

Name _____

 **Thinking About the Writer's Purpose**—*Tales such as this one have been told for generations to entertain listeners and readers. Even though entertainment is the storyteller's primary purpose, a good story will also inform and teach.*

1. **What parts of the story did you find the most funny or entertaining?**

   _____

   _____

2. **The story also is informative. What new animals did you learn about when you read the story?**

   _____

   _____

3. **The story also teaches a lesson about behavior. When Tiddalik is greedy and takes all the water for himself, what happens to the rest of the world?**

   _____

   _____

4. **What does this story teach you about sharing?**

   _____

   _____

5. **Think about the animals' plan to make Tiddalik give up the water. Why do you think they chose to make Tiddalik laugh rather than to hurt him?**

   _____

   _____

   _____

6. **What does the story teach you about solving problems?**

   _____

   _____

Name _____

# Bicycles to Airplanes

**Building Context: Scanning and Predicting**—*A good reader often reads the same story several times to understand it better. Sometimes every word is not read. Instead, the reader will quickly read or* **scan** *the title and the first sentence of each paragraph. The reader looks for key words in order to have a general idea of a story's main points. A reader will also begin* **predicting** *or making guesses about the story and its characters.*

You are going to read the story of the Wright Brothers, the team who built the first successful airplane.

**1.** What does the title of the story, "Bicycles to Airplanes," suggest to you?

  **a.** The brothers rode bikes and then flew planes.

  **b.** Building bicycles helped the brothers know how to build airplanes.

  **c.** The brothers rode bicycles to the airport.

**2.** How much education do you think the Wright Brothers had?

  **a.** They both earned engineering degrees from college.

  **b.** They were high school graduates with technical training.

  **c.** They were high school dropouts.

**3.** Wilbur believed that for a flying machine to be successful, it would need three parts. What do you think these three parts are?

  _____   _____   _____

**4.** Describe the kind of place you think the brothers would pick to test their flying machine.

  _____

  _____

**5.** How long do you think a flying machine would have to stay in the air for the flight to be considered a success?

  _____

  _____

Read Orville and Wilbur's story. Then see how correct your predictions were.

Scholastic Teaching Resources

**Reading the Story**

When four-year-old Wilbur welcomed his little brother Orville into the family, no one suspected that the two boys would grow up to form one of the most famous and successful teams in history, the Wright Brothers.

While the boys read many of the books in their father's library, neither one finished high school. Wilbur was injured during a skating accident and stayed home to recover and to take care of his sick mother. Orville was an average student, but he quit school to start a printing business.

Wilbur joined Orville in building a printing press out of an old tombstone and buggy parts. They did small printing jobs and published their own newspaper. Then in 1893 the Wright Brothers opened a bicycle shop. They built, sold, and repaired bicycles. Their knowledge of bicycles helped them when they decided to try to build an airplane.

Wilbur was the one who first became interested in flying. He read everything he could find about flying and came up with his own ideas for a flying machine. He decided it would need wings, an engine, and a control system. Wilbur's control system is what set him apart from all others who were trying to build flying machines. He built his system out of old bicycle parts, and when he tested it on a small kite, it worked.

In 1900 Wilbur and Orville began building and testing gliders at Kitty Hawk in North Carolina. They picked this spot because the air was windy and the ground was sandy. The wind would help the gliders stay in the air, and the sand would help soften their landings. Once the brothers built a good glider, they were ready to add an engine to build a real flying machine. When no one would build the kind of engine they wanted, they built it themselves in their bicycle shop.

In December 1903 the Wright Brothers were ready to test their flying machine at Kitty Hawk. Wilbur was the pilot. He stalled the engine and crashed. After some repairs to the plane, Orville made the next attempt to fly on December 17, 1903, and he succeeded! The flight lasted only 12 seconds, and the plane went only 120 feet, but it worked! It was the first heavier-than-air machine-powered flight in the world. Now the world of flight was opened up for people. In time, there would be bigger and better planes and jets and even space shuttles. It all began with two brothers working in their bicycle shop.

Name _____

 **Thinking About the Writer's Purpose**

In this story, the writer's main purpose is to give you information about these two famous inventors.

**1.** What in the Wright Brothers' background do you think helped them when they built their gliders and flying machines?

_____

_____

_____

**2.** What might have discouraged the Wright Brothers as they tried to build a working airplane?

_____

_____

_____

**3.** The writer also tries to make the story entertaining by including some interesting facts about the Wright Brothers. Give three examples of facts in the story that you found interesting or surprising.

_____

_____

_____

**4.** When people were able to fly, what were some of the changes that took place in the world?

_____

_____

_____

**5.** What can you learn from the story of the Wright Brothers that can help you in your own life?

_____

_____

_____

Scholastic Teaching Resources

# The Wright Brothers

### Practicing Reading Aloud

Good readers are often called upon to read aloud for a class or for a special occasion. Before reading in front of an audience, a good reader will prepare by following several steps.

1. **Read the piece through, so the subject is understood.**

   **On page 35, there is a poem about the Wright Brothers for you to read aloud. You have read the story of the Wright Brothers, so this poem's subject is one you already know something about.**

2. **Check to make sure you know the meaning of, and how to pronounce, all the words.**

   **Here are some of the longer words used in the poem. Practice reading them a few times, so you can say them smoothly and quickly.**

   | | |
   |---|---|
   | brothers | launched |
   | airplane | bicycle |
   | perfected | man-powered |

3. **Notice how punctuation is used because that will determine how the piece is read.**

   **A comma (,) indicates a place where the reader pauses briefly.**

   **A period (.) indicates a longer pause.**

   **A question mark (?) indicates the voice rises at the end of a line.**

   **An exclamation point (!) indicates the reader's voice should show excitement.**

Practice reading these sentences aloud, paying attention to the punctuation.

1. **Two brothers, Orville and Wilbur, built the first successful airplane.**

2. **How do you think they did it?**

3. **The flight lasted only 12 seconds, but it worked! People could fly!**

Name _____

➡️ **Practicing Reading Aloud**

## The Wright Brothers

There once were two brothers
Named Orville and Will,
And they launched the first airplane,
From Kill Devil Hill.

The flight was a short one
No more than a hop,
In a plane they had made
In their bicycle shop.

But when it was over,
Those brothers named Wright,
Had perfected the airplane,
And man-powered flight!

—Helen H. Moore

*Why do you think the poet calls Wilbur "Will" in the second line?*

_____

_____

*Circle the two commas in the first verse. These are places where you will pause briefly when you read.*

*"Kill Devil Hill" was a specific place on the outer banks of North Carolina near Kitty Hawk.*

*There is only one pause in this verse of the poem after the word* hop. *Circle the comma, so you are sure to notice it when you read.*

*The last verse is a very important one because it tells of Orville and Wilbur's great achievement. Notice how the poet wants you to read this verse more slowly. There is a short pause after three of the lines, and at the end there is an exclamation point. As you read, let your voice build up to this last line. Then read it with force.*

Scholastic Teaching Resources

Practice reading the poem aloud several times. Then read it for a family member.

# Waiting Out Winter

**Building Context and Vocabulary**

Think about how you would behave if it was very cold. Imagine the winds are blowing and snow is falling. What would you do to make sure your house was warm and cozy?

_____

_____

How would you dress if you had to go outside?

_____

_____

What kinds of food sound good to eat on a cold wintry day?

_____

_____

Now think about what a cold winter would be like if you had no house and no clothes. What would you eat if the only food you had was what you could find in the woods? Think about what winter must be like for the animals.

Here are some of the names of the animals you will be reading about. Practice reading them.

| | | |
|---|---|---|
| **squirrels** | **mice** | **rabbits** |
| **rodents** | **foxes** | **deer** |
| **weasels** | **birds** | **chipmunks** |
| **bears** | **skunks** | **Monarch butterflies** |

There are two new words in the story that the writer will explain as you read. See if you can guess what they mean before you read about them.

**migrate** _____

_____

**hibernation** _____

_____

Name _____

 **Reading the Story**

In the winter when it grows very cold and snow covers the ground, you have to make some changes in your life. You do not play outside as much when the cold winds are blowing. Instead, you stay in a warm house and play games, read books, and watch television. You cannot wear shorts and sandals in the wintertime. When you do go out, you wear a heavy coat, gloves, and boots. There are no more picnics when the weather turns cold. Soup and hot chocolate taste best on wintry days.

Did you ever wonder what animals do during winter? Animals do not have warm houses or stores where they can buy heavy clothes and hot food, but, like you, they must make changes in the winter.

Animals find special shelters in the winter to protect them from the cold. Squirrels, mice, and rabbits find holes in trees and logs or even burrow underground. Their fur grows thicker in the winter to help keep them warm. Some animals, like rabbits and weasels, grow special white fur, so they can hide in the snow. Even the animals' food is different in the winter. Rabbits and deer have to eat twigs, tree bark, and moss because there are no green plants. Red foxes eat insects and fruit during the warm months but in the cold winter must hunt small rodents for food.

Did you ever wish you could just leave during the winter and take a long vacation in someplace warm? Well, some animals do just that. They *migrate*. That means they travel to someplace warm where they can find food. Many birds migrate in the fall. Monarch butterflies also migrate and spend the winter in sunny Mexico.

Sometimes on a very cold morning when the wind is howling, you may want to snuggle under the covers and just stay in bed. Some animals spend part or all of the winter in a special, deep sleep called *hibernation*. Bears, skunks, and chipmunks eat a lot of extra food in the fall and store up fat in their bodies. Then in the winter, they curl up and hibernate until the weather turns warm.

**Noticing Patterns: Comparing and Contrasting—**_Writers usually follow a plan when they write. One pattern is comparing and contrasting. To_ **compare** _is to identify similarities and to_ **contrast** _is to identify differences. Understanding the pattern makes a story easier to read and understand._

One pattern that is used in "Waiting Out Winter" is comparing and contrasting. The writer talks about what people do in the winter and then compares that to what animals do. Complete the following chart using the comparisons the writer makes.

| People | Animals |
|---|---|
| People stay in warm houses. | |
| | Animals grow thicker fur. |
| | Rabbits and deer eat twigs, bark, and moss. Foxes eat rodents. |
| People go on vacation to places that are warm. | |
| People snuggle under the covers and stay in bed a little longer on cold mornings. | |

Name _____

# Bear

 **Reading Aloud With Expression**

You have read about the different ways people and animals spend their winters. Now read a poem about two characters: a child and a bear. Each seems very happy not to be like the other.

Remember to pay attention to punctuation. This poem has four exclamation points, so you need to show a lot of emotion. There is only one comma where you will pause slightly, but you should also pause after the colons (:) and dashes (—).

Notice, too, that each verse begins with a "tag." A tag is the part of a sentence that tells who is speaking. Read the tags in the voice of a narrator and then use different voices for each of the two characters.

## Bear

Once a child said:
"I wouldn't like to be a bear—
I couldn't stand being covered with hair!
But the thing I'd really hate—
Would be to have to hibernate!"

Once a bear replied:
"I wouldn't like to be a child—
I like it out here, in the wild!
And the thing I'd really hate—
Is, children
Never
Hibernate!"

—Helen H. Moore

*How old do you think this child is?*

_____

*The child is talking about something he or she does not like. Describe how you think the child's voice should sound.*

_____

_____

_____

*Do you think this bear likes children? Why or why not?*

_____

_____

_____

*Describe how you think the bear's voice should sound.*

_____

_____

Name _____

# The Bat, the Birds, and the Beasts

**Reading With Expression**—*Stories that have dialogue are more interesting and lively if they are read with expression.* **Dialogue** *is the part of the sentence that tells what a character or characters are saying. Dialogue is always set off by quotation marks (" "). Usually a tag will introduce dialogue. A tag is the part of a sentence that tells who is speaking and sometimes how the dialogue should be spoken.*

Here are some examples of sentences from the story "The Bat, the Birds, and the Beasts." Read each sentence. Then circle the tag and underline the dialogue.

**"Why are you here?" the beasts asked.**

**"Not me!" cried the bat.**

**"From now on you must fly alone at night," they said.**

Draw an *X* by the sentence that should be read with a lot of excitement.

Draw a star by the sentence that asks a question.

Notice that one of the sentences has the tag "said." That tag does not give the reader a clue about how to read the sentence. However, a good reader can pick up clues from the story to help decide what expression to use. In this story, "they" are animals who are angry at the bat. Read that sentence as though you were speaking for a bunch of angry animals.

Before you read the story, think about what characteristics a bat has.

**How is a bat like a bird?** _____

_____

**How is a bat like an animal?** _____

_____

Now read about how the bat made the birds and animals angry.

**Reading the Story**

Once there was a great war between the birds and the beasts. At first, Bat was on the birds' side, but when he saw they were losing the fight, he crawled under a log and hid. When the beasts began celebrating their victory, Bat crawled out and joined them. "Why are you here?" the beasts asked. "You were helping the birds."

"Not me!" cried Bat. "Why would I help those silly creatures? I am not a bird. Look in my mouth. See my teeth. No bird has teeth." So the beasts said nothing and let Bat stay with them.

The next day the fighting began again, and this time the beasts were losing. Again, Bat crept away and hid until the fighting was over. When the birds began celebrating their victory, Bat crawled out and joined them. "Why are you here?" the birds asked. "You were helping the beasts."

"Not me!" cried Bat. "Why would I help those silly creatures? I am not a beast. Look at my wings. No beast has wings." So the birds said nothing and let Bat stay with them.

All through the war, Bat kept switching sides. When the beasts were winning, Bat joined the beasts. When the birds were winning, Bat joined the birds.

Finally, tired of all the fighting, the birds and beasts declared peace. Both sides joined together to celebrate the end of the war. When Bat tried to join the celebration, both the birds and the beasts chased him away. "From now on you must fly around alone at night," they said. "Since you could be neither one thing nor the other, you can have no friends."

Scholastic Teaching Resources

Name _____

## The Bat, the Birds, and the Beasts

 **Reading Aloud With Expression**

The story of "The Bat, the Birds, and the Beasts can be rewritten as a play with the following parts: the beasts, the bat, and a narrator.

Practice reading the parts while being sure to make your voice show the different feelings of the characters.

**Narrator:** Once there was a great war between the birds and the beasts. At first, Bat was on the birds' side, but when he saw they were losing the fight, he crawled under a log and hid. When the beasts began celebrating their victory, Bat crawled out and joined them.

**Beasts:** "Why are you here?"

**Narrator:** the beasts asked.

**Beasts:** "You were helping the birds."

**Bat:** "Not me!"

**Narrator:** cried Bat.

**Bat:** "Why would I help those silly creatures? I am not a bird. Look in my mouth. See my teeth. No bird has teeth."

**Narrator:** So the beasts said nothing and let Bat stay with them. The next day the fighting began again, and this time, the beasts were losing. Again, Bat crept away and hid until the fighting was over. When the birds began celebrating their victory, Bat crawled out and joined them.

*The narrator should be sure to pay attention to the punctuation. Remember, you need a short pause when there is a comma and longer pauses for periods.*

*Since the beasts saw the bat helping the birds, how do you think they feel when they see him now on their side?*

    *a. angry*

    *b. confused*

    *c. grateful*

*The readers' voices should show the emotion you picked.*

*Now Bat does not want to get caught by either side. Describe how you think he should sound.*

_____

_____

_____

*Remember, the narrator should watch for commas and periods, so there are pauses that help the listeners follow along with the story.*

Scholastic Teaching Resources

**Birds:** "Why are you here?"

**Narrator:** the birds asked.

**Birds:** "You were helping the beasts."

**Bat:** "Not me!"

**Narrator:** cried Bat.

**Bat:** "Why would I help those silly creatures? I am not a beast. Look at my wings. No beast has wings."

**Narrator:** So the birds said nothing and let Bat stay with them.

All through the war, Bat kept switching sides. When the beasts were winning, Bat joined the beasts. When the birds were winning, Bat joined the birds.

Finally, tired of all the fighting, the birds and beasts declared peace. Both sides joined together to celebrate the end of the war. When Bat tried to join the celebration, both the birds and the beasts chased him away.

**Birds and Beasts:** "From now on you must fly around alone at night,"

**Narrator:** they said.

**Birds and Beasts:** "Since you could be neither one thing nor the other, you can have no friends."

*What emotion did you think the beasts had when they asked Bat this question?*

_____

*Use this emotion here for the birds.*

*How did you decide to have the tricky bat sound?*

_____

_____

*Make him sound that way here, too.*

*Bat keeps jumping back and forth changing sides. Practice reading this so the narrator's voice helps the reader to see what a shifty character Bat is.*

*Now the birds and beast are on to Bat's trick, and they are angry with him. Be sure the speakers' voices show this anger.*

Name _____

# Potter's Pets

 **Building Context and Predicting**

Have you ever read the story of Flopsy, Mopsy, Cottontail, and Peter? They are all characters in *The Tale of Peter Rabbit*. Beatrix Potter published this book in England in 1902, and it became one of the most famous stories ever written.

Did you ever wonder where writers and artists get ideas for their stories and drawings? You are going to read about Beatrix Potter. The title of the story "Potter's Pets" gives you a good guess about what gave her ideas. She used her own pets as characters in her stories and models for her drawings.

Here are some of the names of characters in Potter's books that were also pets she owned. See if you can match the pet with the character name. (Hint: Potter loved rabbits, so two of the characters are rabbits.)

____ **Mrs. Tiggy-winkle**      **a. pig**

____ **Benjamin**      **b. hedgehog**

____ **Pig-Wig**      **c. rabbit**

____ **Peter**

You will also come across some unfamiliar words in the story. Practice reading the underlined words. Then see if you can guess what the words mean by how they are used in the sentences. Write the letter of the correct definition of the word on the blank before the sentence.

____ **1. Potter's parents were <u>overprotective</u> and did not allow Beatrix and her brother to keep company with other children.**

**a. drawing quickly**

**b. extremely cautious and careful**

____ **2. So they played with each other and a <u>menagerie</u> of pets.**

**c. a collection**

____ **3. She brought rabbits, mice, and hedgehogs into her house and spent long hours playing with them and <u>sketching</u> their pictures.**

**Reading the Story**

In 1893 Beatrix Potter wrote a picture letter to the young son of her former governess. The five-year-old boy was sick in bed, and she wanted to cheer him up with the story of four little rabbits: Flopsy, Mopsy, Cottontail, and Peter. In 1902 the story of these four rabbits was published in a book called *The Tale of Peter Rabbit*, which became one of the most popular children's books of all time. Over the years, Potter continued to write and illustrate children's books. Nearly all of the characters in her books are based on the pets she had throughout her life.

Potter's parents were overprotective and did not allow Beatrix and her brother to keep company with other children. So they played with each other and a menagerie of pets. Especially after her brother, Bertram, was sent away to boarding school, Potter turned to her pets for company. She brought rabbits, mice, and hedgehogs into her house and spent long hours playing with them and sketching their pictures.

Potter's first pet rabbit was named Benjamin. She bought him at a London pet shop and sneaked him home in a paper bag. Potter said that Benjamin loved to eat hot buttered toast and would hurry into the room when he heard the bell for tea. Later, Potter actually had a rabbit named Peter. Peter was a very clever rabbit and learned many tricks. She taught him to jump through a hoop, to ring a bell, and to play the tambourine. Potter used Benjamin and Peter as models for many of her drawings of rabbits in her books.

Another character in Potter's books was Mrs. Tiggy-winkle, a hedgehog. Potter also had a pet hedgehog by the same name that she used to take with her on trips. She once wrote to a friend that Mrs. Tiggy-winkle loved to travel by train and would drink milk from a doll's teacup.

Even after Potter grew up, she loved animals. With the money she earned from her books, she bought a farm and became an expert in raising sheep. She kept sheepdogs and other animals as well. Potter bought a little black pig that could not be kept with the other pigs at her farm. Potter kept the pig in a basket by the side of her bed and fed it from a bottle. The little pig became so attached to Potter that it followed her everywhere. Little Pig-Wig became another of the characters in Potter's books.

**Thinking About the Story**

1. The main purpose of this story is to give you information about Beatrix Potter. The writer knows that not everything about Beatrix Potter's life can be told in only one page. Which sentence in the first paragraph tells you what part of Potter's life the writer will focus on?

_____

_____

_____

_____

2. Why do you think Beatrix Potter loved animals so much?

_____

_____

_____

_____

3. What four examples of pets does the writer give in the story?

_____

4. In addition to giving you information, the writer tries to make the story entertaining by giving you interesting details about Potter's pets. Give two examples of details that you thought were interesting or entertaining.

_____

_____

_____

_____

5. Think about a pet that you or that someone you know has had. On another sheet of paper, write a short story in which that pet is the main character. Draw a picture of the pet. Who knows? You might be as lucky as Beatrix Potter and have a bestseller.

# Answer Key

## Page 4
1. star, famous, celebrity; 2. popularity;
3. circus, train; 4. London; 5. Canada,
United States; 6. Natural History
Museum; 7. Tufts University; elephant

## Page 5
some, thing; show, man; rail, road;
every, one; any, thing; 1. Color *United
States*, *London*, and *Canada* red.
2. Color *track*, *railroad*, and *tunnels*
yellow. 3. Color *millions*, *largest*, *tons*,
and *hundred* blue. 4. circus, zoo;
5. accident, tragedy, skeleton;
6. Outline *anything*, *showman*, and
*railroad* in green.

## Page 7
1. Accept all reasonable answers.
2. *Peak* means "the greatest level."
3. Accept all reasonable answers.

## Page 8
1. good; 2. not good; 3. not good;
4. good; Answers will vary.

## Page 9

## Page 11
1. premature, sickly; 2. segregation;
3. polio, deformed; Answers may vary.
Possible answers include: her
mother—did not give up, found a black
medical college; her brothers and
sisters—helped her exercise; her
coaches—invited her to attend a
summer camp

## Page 12
water, fall; a. not allowing; b. a risky
act; c. one who takes risks; d. an
unexplainable event; e. the very edge

## Page 15
1. Answers will vary. 2. Possible
answers include: Their trips were
different because Miss Taylor was in
an oak barrel while Roger was in a life
jacket. Miss Taylor's trip was planned,
but Roger's trip was an accident. Their
trips were similar because both
survived and only suffered minor
injuries.

## Page 17
guide dog

## Page 18
Answers will vary. Possible answers
include: Daisy, both, both, both, both,
both, both

## Page 20
Daisy had to learn basic commands.
She also had to learn to always pay
close attention and not to be
distracted.

Ann had to learn different commands
using her voice and body movements.

They were able to practice walking
together when they could
communicate with each other.

## Page 24
Answers may vary. Possible answers
include: 1. Tom could not believe how
bright electric lights can be. It was the
first time the Olympic Games were
held in the United States. Tom and his
family saw a new invention called a
"moving picture." Tom and his family
tried new foods such as hot dogs, iced
tea, and ice-cream cones.
2. A "moving picture" is a movie.
3. Answers will vary. 4. a concrete
stadium; a "moving picture," hot dogs,
iced tea, peanut butter, ice-cream
cones

## Page 25
1. aluminum, plastic, paper, glass;
2. California, Texas, New York; Texas
should be circled. 3. landfill

## Page 28
1. It persuades the reader to recycle
aluminum, glass, plastic, and paper.
2. clean, resources; 3. Answers will
vary. Check facts. 4. Answers will vary.
Check examples.

## Page 29
1. f; 2. a; 3. g; 4. b; 5. d; 6. c; 7. e

## Page 31
3. The plants and trees began to die.
The other animals became thirsty.

## Page 34
Possible answers include: 1. They built
a printing press themselves. They also
built, sold, and repaired bicycles.
2. No one would build the kind of
engine they wanted. 3-5. Answers will
vary.

## Page 37
Possible answers include: migrate—to
move from place to place;
hibernation—the process of sleeping
during the winter

## Page 39
People: People stay in warm houses.
People wear heavy coats, gloves, and
hats. People eat soup and drink hot
chocolate. People go on vacation to
places that are warm. People snuggle
under the covers and stay in bed a
little longer on cold mornings.
Animals: Squirrels, mice, and rabbits
find holes in trees and logs and even
burrow underground. Animals grow
thicker fur. Rabbits and deer eat twigs,
bark, and moss. Foxes eat rodents.
Some animals migrate to warmer
places. Some animals spend part of
the winter in a deep sleep called
*hibernation*.

## Page 41
"Why are you here?"
the beasts asked., "Not me!"
cried the bat., "From now on you must
fly alone at night," they said.; Draw an
X by "Not me!" cried the bat. Draw a
star by "Why are you here? the beasts
asked. Answers will vary. Possible
answers include: Bats have wings and
can fly. Bats are furry and have fingers
and toes.

## Page 45
b, c, a, c; 1. b; 2. c; 3. a

## Page 47
1. Nearly all the characters in her
books are based on the pets she had
throughout her life. 2. Answers will
vary. Possible answers include: She
and her brother played with a
menagerie of pets to keep them
company. 3. rabbits, mice, a hedgehog,
pig; 4. Answers will vary.

Scholastic Professional Books

Scholastic Teaching Resources